G000122733

SITUATIONS

Stories for Assembly and P.S.E.

Gordon Aspland

SOUTHGATE

Copyright © Gordon Aspland 1997
Copyright © Illustrations Southgate Publishers Ltd

First published 1997 by Southgate Publishers Ltd

Southgate Publishers Ltd
15 Barnfield Avenue, Exmouth, Devon EX8 2QE

All rights reserved. No part of this publication may be reproduced, copied or transmitted in any form or by any means, electronic, mechanical, photocopying, recording or otherwise, without the prior written permission of the publisher or in accordance with the Copyright, Design and Patents Act 1988.

Printed and bound in Great Britain by Short Run Press Ltd, Exeter, Devon.

British Library Cataloguing in Publication Data
A CIP catalogue record for this book is available from the British Library.

ISBN 1–85741–043–2

Acknowledgements:
The publishers would like to thank Chris Lee, Rolle Faculty of Education, University of Plymouth for his advice.

CONTENTS

SITUATIONS

Introduction

Throughout our lives we find ourselves in difficult situations. We have to make decisions about what to do. Adults have a wealth of lifetime experiences to help them and even then often get it wrong! Children need to be given opportunities to explore the issues and factors that affect their decisions.

Situations is the third book in this series, following *Choices* and *Feelings*. With *Situations* I have tried to look at children's choices between different courses of action. In some cases there are obvious right and wrong decisions and in others the demarcation between right and wrong is not so obvious. The situations are developed around issues that affect many children, such as temptation, bullying, peer group pressure and unfairness. The stories are designed to stimulate children to think about and discuss the courses of action available. It is hoped that through this process of listening and thinking and putting views forward, children will begin to understand how their own actions affect themselves and others.

All the stories are based around a group of children in the same class. The adults also remain the same. By this means I hope that listeners can build up a picture of the characters and their personalities as the stories are told. They might identify with one or more of them.

I believe that these stories reflect some of the moral values described in the N.C.C. Document on *Spiritual and Moral Development (1993)*. These include: telling the truth; keeping promises; respecting the rights and property of others; acting considerately towards each other; helping those less fortunate and weaker than ourselves; taking personal responsibility for one's actions; and self-discipline.

SUGGESTIONS FOR USE

In Collective Worship
This book can be picked up and the stories used just as they are by the teacher in a hurry. They take between five and fifteen minutes to read and, with a short follow-up

discussion, song or hymn and prayer or silent reflection, they would occupy an assembly for collective worship of between fifteen and twenty minutes. More satisfactory than this is the planning of episodes from the book into a full-term pattern of collective worship, alongside religious material from Christianity and other world faiths, so that Tuesday, say, might be the day for these stories, with other things happening on the other days. This would provide a coherent framework in which to set these 'broadly Christian' but essentially secular stories which would meet the requirement of the Education Reform Act that, taking a term as a whole, the collective worship must be wholly or mainly of a broadly Christian nature.

After each story I have provided questions for discussion and a prayer which can be introduced in an open-ended way by phrases like 'We're going to have a few quiet moments to think about ... ' As well as using the story in collective worship, some teachers might want to use some of the follow-up activities suggested in class.

In Classwork

Within the National Curriculum framework the stories might be used particularly in oral work in P.S.E. and English.

1. In pairs, the children can discuss the story. The teacher then asks one child to relate how their partner feels. This is a simple but effective way of encouraging listening as well as talking.

2. The children can be asked to write down a response to the story or how they think it should end and then discuss what they have written in a small group. A variation on this is to split the class in half. One half sits in a circle facing outwards and the other half forms a circle facing inwards, so that each is facing someone from the inner circle. The teacher can then ask questions about the story or the children's response and the children discuss in pairs. After each question, the children in the outer circle move round so that they are facing somebody new. This encourages children to talk to someone they might not normally relate to.

3. Some stories have a natural break in the middle for questions and discussion about the choices the character can make.

By using the Discussion questions after each story and the oral work mentioned above, children can start to develop P.S.E. skills such as: predicting outcomes from different types of behaviour; empathizing with other people's feelings; reflecting on their own behaviour and feelings; and respecting the views and feelings of others.

The sub-title of this book sums up its intention — to provide stories for Assembly and P.S.E., born out of my own work with children in the upper part of the primary school. I hope it will help other teachers in their work.

Gordon Aspland
1997

1
Bess Saves the Day

THEME: looking after our pets

Jonny loved his pet dog, Bess. She was the smallest of the litter and the last to be sold. Jonny and his parents couldn't resist her. Bess was half Jack Russell and half Border Collie, though she looked more like a long-legged Jack Russell with large ears and a big bushy tail. She loved people and followed Jonny around the house wherever he went. When Jonny arrived home from school Bess would be waiting and Jonny couldn't wait to see her. She would come bounding up to him jumping up as if her legs had springs. Most children would turn the TV on as soon as they got home from school, but not Jonny. He would grab a tennis ball and go outside to play with Bess. He did everything for her, preparing her dinner, grooming her, taking her for walks and even cleaning up the little messes she used to make when she was a puppy. Bess was Jonny's dog, Bess would do whatever he said. Yes, Jonny loved his dog, and one day something very strange happened that enabled Bess to show how much she loved him.

Jonny was about to take Bess for a walk to the park when his mother stopped him. "Jonny, would you be a dear and put these papers in the paper bank for me?" she asked. She handed him the bag in such a way that said he had no choice so he took the bag and left the house. The park was a few blocks away and at the entrance were two large containers, one for paper and one for bottles. He walked up to the paper bank with Bess at his side. He usually walked Bess on a lead when they were by a road but then took her off when they got to the park. He leaned down to unhook Bess's lead, he then coiled it into his hand. Bess immediately began to sniff for nice smells around the bottle bank while Jonny took the newspapers out of the plastic bag and began to throw them into the paper bank. He was only just able to reach the square opening as he tipped the paper into the black hole. He then picked up the bag and stuffed it into his pocket, called Bess and began to walk around the park.

Jonny and Bess played their usual games of hiding behind trees and jumping out on each other. Soon Jonny was back at the entrance to the park and he felt in

his pocket for Bess's lead. He couldn't find it! Where on earth was it? He must have dropped it in the park. It was bright red so it would be easy to see. Jonny began to trot around looking for it. Bess tried hiding behind trees again but she was disappointed when Jonny wouldn't play this time. He quickly ran around the park but he couldn't find the lead. He stood at the entrance again and tried to think of what he had done with it. He remembered holding the lead in his hand when he was putting the newspapers into the paper bank. The paper bank! He must have accidentally thrown it into the bank. He ran over to it. He tried to see into the hole but it was too high up for him to look into. He grabbed onto the side and hoisted himself up. Hanging on, he was now able to look inside and, as his eyes became used to the dim light inside, he could see part of the lead under a newspaper. He moved his position so that his head and shoulders were in the opening and he carefully leaned in to try and reach the lead. It was just out of his reach so he shuffled forward a little more and tried again. He just got his fingers onto the lead when he felt himself go forward, lose his balance and fall into the big dark container! As he landed awkwardly onto his side, he felt a sharp pain in his arm. He lay still for a moment, not believing what he had done. He closed his eyes and then opened them again, hoping that it was all a dream. But no, he was stuck in a dark metal hole, which smelt of old newspapers. His arm began to throb but when he tried to move he could feel a sharp pain in his elbow so he lay very still. What should he do? *We are thankful for our pets, for how they enrich our lives and for the friendship they give.*

How can Jonny try to attract attention in order to get help?

Meanwhile, outside, Bess was waiting patiently for her lead to be put on. She was puzzled when Jonny began to climb up to the newspaper bank and was very surprised when he disappeared inside. She didn't know where he had gone and she began to whine with anxiety. Her ears perked up when she heard Jonny's voice from inside the container. He was calling her name. She ran over to the bank and tried jumping up to the hole but it was much too high for her. Jonny was calling, "Help Bess, help!" Bess knew he was in trouble and she began to bark and bark like she had never barked before. She wasn't going to leave Jonny, so she tried to attract attention by making a lot of noise.

It was the Park Keeper who noticed Bess barking. He walked over to her but because she was barking so much he didn't hear Jonny calling for help. He grabbed Bess's collar and tried to drag her towards his van. He thought she was a stray and he was going to take her to the dogs' home. But Bess was desperate, she managed to scrabble away. She ran back to the paper bank and barked again. The Park Keeper was very surprised at her behaviour. This time he approached Bess with caution, thinking that she might turn nasty. Then he heard Jonny calling. At first he couldn't tell where the voice was coming from. It was Bess scratching the side of the bank trying to get in that told him that the voice was coming from inside the container. He dashed over to the hole, looked down and saw Jonny.

"What on earth are you doing there? Don't answer that question, I'll get you out first." The opening for the newspaper bank was quite big so the Park Keeper was able to climb into the container. He carefully lowered himself down beside Jonny. "Have you hurt yourself?" he asked.

"My elbow hurts," whimpered Jonny.

The Park Keeper examined Jonny's arm. "I think you've dislocated your elbow, young man. Here's what we'll do." The Park Keeper unzipped Jonny's jacket. Then he carefully placed Jonny's bad arm inside the jacket and zipped it up so that the jacket was supporting Jonny's arm.

While he was doing this another head appeared at the opening of the container. "Hey, Joe, what are you doing in there, having a tea party?" It was the Park Keeper's friend who had come to meet him at the gate.

"I'm glad to see you Ron. You can help me with this young man," Joe answered. He carefully lifted Jonny to the opening of the container. Jonny winced with pain but he was determined not to cry out. Ron took hold of Jonny and pulled him out of the newspaper bank. When he lowered him to the ground Bess leapt onto Jonny and showered him with kisses. Joe scrambled out of the container, rather red in the face and puffing hard.

"Now young man, perhaps you can tell me how you managed to find yourself in there," he demanded.

Discussion Points

1. How does Jonny show that he loves Bess?
2. Why do people keep pets?
3. How would a dog react to someone who was cruel to them?

Prayer/Reflection

When we treat our pets with kindness and love they will reward us with their trust and affection. If we treat them with cruelty and do not look after them properly they will distrust us and be hostile towards us. We are thankful for our pets, for how they enrich our lives and for the friendship they give.

Follow-up Activities

1. Ask the children to describe, either orally or in writing, what Jonny said to the Park Keeper.
2. Look at the different ways we look after various pets.
3. Let the children design a 'pets charter' in order to encourage others to look after their pets properly.

2
Friends No More

THEME: saying cruel things to other people

George Hammond was a bully. He had been a bully for many years and, unless he changed his ways, he would be a bully for many more. Unfortunately for Clare White, he lived next door to her. He hadn't been a bully at first. He and Clare were born within a few months of each other and their mothers had been good friends. When they were toddlers their mothers would get together for morning coffee and put toys on the floor for the two children to play with. Their mothers were pleased when the two children started school at the same time and were in the same class. At that time George and Clare played well together and they, too, were happy to be in the same class. After all, it is nice to have a familiar face in the class when you first start school. But George changed and things were never the same again.

It was around the time when George and Clare moved into the Juniors that George changed. He had always been a bit silly and in order to gain attention he was naughty. When he got into the Juniors he became a bully as well. Things were not very happy at home and perhaps this was the only way he could get other people to pay attention to him. He didn't actually physically hurt anybody, it was what he said that upset them. He poked fun at the clothes they wore, he teased children for wearing glasses or a brace. He swore at other children and when they complained to Mrs Hatch, their teacher, he pleaded innocence. He was very crafty because he never got caught being horrible to others.

He was particularly beastly to Clare. Clare's mother banned him from playing at their house because of his swearing and nastiness. George's mother wasn't happy about this and she stopped speaking to Clare's mother. George continued to say horrid things in order to upset Clare when they were at school. Clare's mother complained to Mrs Hatch and she made sure that they were not sitting at the same table. But even that didn't stop George, he just kept on at Clare at playtimes. It got to the point when Clare did not want to go to school. Whenever Mrs Hatch or Mr Hall confronted George he would plead innocence and pretend that

near each other.

it was the other children being horrible to him. George's mother wouldn't believe he was like that and she told Mr Hall that the other children bullied George.

One day George was feeling particularly nasty. They were doing maths and George was getting bored. Actually, George didn't have a clue about the work he had to do. He stared at the sums in his book. They didn't make any sense to him at all. He looked around the classroom. Mrs Hatch was busy working with another group of children. George noticed Clare working by the measuring table so he got

up and sneaked over to her. When he was beside her he whispered something in her ear that made her face drain of blood. Tears swelled in her eyes and she suddenly burst into tears.

"I heard that, George!" George spun around. Mrs Holden, the classroom assistant, was standing right behind him. He hadn't noticed her because she was bending over, searching in a cupboard. The class went quiet. George bit his lip.

"I didn't say anything," he said in a worried voice.

Mrs Hatch came over and asked, "What's this all about, Mrs Holden?"

"This nasty little boy said something to Clare that really upset her," she announced.

"I didn't, she's been nasty to me," shouted George.

"Clare was minding her own business and you came over and said a horrible thing to her. Anybody would be upset to hear what you said," replied Mrs Holden.

"Well, what did he say?" asked Mrs Hatch. The rest of the class went quiet, they wanted to know as well.

What do you think George might have said to upset Clare so much?

Mrs Holden took a big breath and told them all, "He said, 'I'm going to kill your rabbit,' that's what he said." George went bright red in the face. He looked down at the floor. He couldn't bear to face the rest of the class.

"What are we going to do with you?" asked Mrs Hatch.

Discussion Points
1. What should be done with George?
2. How do you think the other children will behave towards George?
3. What should you do if someone is unpleasant to you? Who can you turn to?

Prayer/Reflection
We can show others what kind of person we are by what we say. Lord, help us to be kind and gentle, to say things that will make people happy.

Follow-up Activities
1. Ask the children to list all the good things we can say about someone, perhaps their writing, painting, performance at sport or personality.
   Then ask them to list some bad things we could say about the above.
   Ask them to think about how the various words make us feel.
   This activity could be done in pairs. To finish, the children could say nice things to their partners.
2. When we see someone is upset what words can we use to make them feel better? Discuss the kinds of words we like to hear when we are upset.

3

They Told Me to Do It

SITUATIONS

THEME: taking responsibility for your own actions

Here are three stories, what do you think they have in common?

STORY 1

There was the usual football game in the playground during lunch time. Jonny, Ganesh and George were kicking a ball around when suddenly it shot up into the air and landed on the PE shed roof.

"Shall I go and get Mr Bell?" asked Ganesh.

"Na, we can get it ourselves," suggested George. "Come on." Looking to see if Mr Bell was watching he led the other two boys to the back of the shed. It was a school rule that children were not allowed behind there. "Jonny and I will help you up," George said to Ganesh.

"I don't want to go up there," said Ganesh.

"You're not afraid are you?" taunted Jonny.

"Alright, help me up." So George and Jonny lifted Ganesh up as high as they could. Ganesh gripped onto the edge of the shed roof and pulled himself on top. The ball was just beyond his finger tips so he wriggled forward. Just as Ganesh got a hand onto the ball a voice boomed out. "What are you doing?" Mr Bell came running over to the shed. "Get down from there this instant," he shouted. Mr Bell went around to the back of the shed and helped Ganesh down. "And now young man, perhaps you can explain to me why you were doing something you are not supposed to be doing?"

Ganesh looked at the others, they were staring at the ground not saying anything. "It wasn't my fault, they told me to do it," he said.

STORY 2

The summer sun beat down. It was too hot to play so the girls were bored. Rafi was thirsty so she went over to the drinking fountain for a drink. Delphine and Clare followed and while Rafi was gulping the water Clare had an idea.

"Rafi, spray us with the water," she said. Rafi looked puzzled at first. "Go on, it'll cool us down," urged Clare. Delphine and Clare stood there, waiting. Rafi grinned and put her finger over the mouth piece of the fountain. Water began to squirt everywhere and the girls were quickly soaked through. Unfortunately for them there was an open window beside the fountain and water sprayed into the classroom. Even more unfortunate for them was that Mrs Hatch's desk was near the window and Mrs Hatch was sitting at her desk marking some books. Water shot through the open window all over the books and all over Mrs Hatch. She jumped out of her seat.

"Stop that this instant! Rafi come here!" Mrs Hatch shouted through the open window.

The girls stopped laughing and Rafi turned to the open window where Mrs Hatch was waiting. "What on earth do you think you are doing, look at the state of you all, you're absolutely soaked. What have you got to say for yourself?"

Rafi looked sheepishly at the others and then she blurted out, "It's not my fault, they told me to do it."

Give us the strength to have the courage to say 'No' when we are tempted to do wrong.

STORY 3

It was a windy, squally day, but everyone breathed a sigh of relief when the weather cleared just enough for the children to go outside. George was in a very grumpy mood. He had been told off by his mum at home. He didn't understand the maths that morning. He got told off for talking by Mrs Hatch and, finally, Jonny had forgotten his football so they had nothing to play with. George was in a real mood.

As they were passing the coat racks to go outside George spotted Delphine's brightly coloured leotard hanging out of her bag. He grabbed it as he walked by and ran outside. Jonny and Ganesh followed him and the three boys began to throw the leotard to each other. There was a shout of "Put that back!" from Delphine as the boys began to play catch with it.

Delphine tried to get it back but the boys kept shouting "Piggy in the middle!" and threw her leotard over her head to each other.

"George Hammond, you're the pig, a big smelly pig," shouted Delphine at George.

Jonny had the leotard at that moment and George shouted to him, "Throw it in there," pointing to a muddy puddle. Jonny stood by the muddy puddle and held the leotard up.

"Don't you dare, Jonny Kirk," warned Delphine.

"Go on, Jonny, drop it," George egged him on. "Pigs like being dirty so she can have a dirty leotard." Jonny looked at George and then he dropped the leotard into the muddy puddle.

Delphine reached forward and retrieved her leotard from the puddle. Through tears she shouted at the boys, "I'm going to Mr Hall," and she ran off into school.

The boys stood around not knowing what to do. Then Mr Hall came out holding the muddy leotard. "Jonny, can you explain to me why this is all muddy?" he asked.

"It wasn't my fault, George told me to do it," said Jonny.

Discussion Points

1. What is the common element among these stories?
2. Who is more to blame, the person who thought of the idea to do wrong, or the others who took part?
3. If someone suggests something to you that you know is wrong what should you do?

Give us the courage to admit when we have done wrong, the grace to apologise & the determination not to make the same mistake again.

Prayer/Reflection

Dear Lord, teach us your wisdom in knowing what is right and wrong. Give us the strength to have the courage to say 'no' when we are tempted to do wrong.

Follow-up Activities

1. Discuss with the children the concept of peer group pressure when they are urged to do something that they know is wrong. Who is to blame? Who should get punished? What should the children in these stories have done to make sure they didn't get into trouble? In pairs children could practice ways of saying 'no' to peers.
2. Groups of children could act these stories out and present them at an assembly for the whole school.

4
The Test

SITUATIONS

Delphine and Rafi were really good friends. They became friends when they were in the playgroup, stayed friends in nursery school and now they were in the same Junior class. They were inseparable. Mrs Hatch allowed them to sit together, in her words, as long they got on with their work and didn't chat. In all subjects they were equal except in one, maths. Rafi found this subject very difficult whereas Delphine had no problems with it. Rafi managed to keep up with her work by copying from Delphine. Delphine didn't mind. After all, Rafi was her best friend. Rafi always managed to fool her teachers that she was good at maths. But then one day she was found out.

Delphine had to go into hospital to have her tonsils out and she was going to be away for at least two weeks. Delphine's parents were hoping she would go in during the holidays but the hospital couldn't manage that. So she had to miss two weeks of school. Delphine was disappointed at this and so was Rafi, her best friend.

Rafi didn't want to go to school on the day Delphine went into hospital. On the way to school she began to worry about who she was going to play with, who she was going to sit beside, and who was going to help her with her maths. Rafi nearly turned around to go home but she realised that her mother would be cross with her so she continued to school.

When Rafi sat down she looked around to see if she could move nearer to her other friend, Clare, but there were no empty seats. Delphine's chair beside her seemed like a big empty space which made her feel very lonely. After morning assembly it was maths, the one lesson Rafi was not looking forward to. She had always had Delphine there to help her. Delphine was very rarely away ill and even when she had one day off for a cold Rafi was lucky because they didn't have maths that day.

The person sitting nearest to Rafi was Jonny and he was in the same maths group as her. They were finishing off a page of maths about decimals. Mrs Hatch told the group on that page to work quietly to the end while she talked to some of the other children. Rafi looked at the next question she had to do. She read it over and over again and no matter how often she read it she still didn't understand what to do. She looked back in her exercise book to see how she had done the previous work. Her work was neat and correct with ticks all down the page and even a 'Good Work' written by Mrs Hatch. But this was work copied from Delphine. Rafi didn't really know how she had done it.

Rafi is feeling very worried. What should she do?

Rafi didn't know what to do. Jonny was busy working away and Rafi craned her neck to see what he was doing. Jonny noticed her looking at his work and quickly covered it up with his hand, whispering "Get off!". Rafi sat for several minutes staring at the questions. She kept looking over at Mrs Hatch to see if she was coming over to her to check on how she was getting on. Rafi's heart raced when she saw Mrs Hatch move away from the group she was working with and start to walk in her direction.

But just then Rafi was literally saved by the bell. Once a term they had fire drill and it was just at that moment when the fire bell began to ring. "Put your pencils

down and line up at the door," said Mrs Hatch. Fire drills always provided a bit of light relief for the children. On this occasion they were particularly noisy and Mr Hall made them do it all again. So by the time the fire drill was finished it was play time and the end of maths. Rafi put her books away with a great feeling of relief, but then Mrs Hatch announced that they were going to have a test the next day!

A test! Rafi couldn't believe her ears. And Delphine wasn't around to help her. All day Rafi kept thinking about the test. That evening she didn't eat her dinner and she asked to go to bed early because she wasn't feeling very well. The next morning she told her mother she had a headache and felt sick and as she hadn't had her dinner the night before, her mother believed her. Rafi spent the day lying on the sofa watching TV. By the end of the day she was feeling better and she announced that she thought she could go to school the next day.

The next day Rafi went to school a little happier as the test was over and they were going on to a new section in their maths book. There were no more fractions to worry about. But Rafi had a shock when Mrs Hatch called her to her desk.

"Rafi, as you weren't here yesterday I would like you to do this test now. You can work in the library area," said Mrs Hatch.

Rafi took the test paper from Mrs Hatch and walked over to the empty desk in the library area. She sat down and stared at the paper. She just didn't know where to start. Tears welled up in her eyes and the figures seemed to dance about the page. She put her pencil down and buried her head.

Clare rushed over to Mrs Hatch to tell her that Rafi was crying. Mrs Hatch got up from her desk and walked up to Rafi. She put her arm around her and asked what was wrong.

"I can't do it," blurted out Rafi in between sobs.

"What do you mean you can't do it? You've been getting your work all right, haven't you?" *Of course you can do it!*

Discussion Points
1. This was the moment of truth for Rafi, what should she say to Mrs Hatch?
2. How did Delphine make it more difficult for Rafi? How could your friends help you?

Prayer/Reflection
Let us be quiet and think about the people who are there to help us, our teachers, classroom assistants, parents and our friends. In God's presence *Let us* we remember that truth is not only about what we say but also what we do.

Follow-up Activities
1. Discuss the various strategies children could use when they are facing difficulties with work.
2. Make a list of all the people who are around to help us.

5
The Broken Finger

THEME: being first is not important

Ganesh was always finishing his work first. He felt some kind of pride that he was the first to have his work marked. During maths he would race ahead of his group, put his pencil down with a satisfied thump and then go and show Mrs Hatch. The other children found this habit really irritating. But they were the ones who were smiling when Ganesh was sent back to his desk with half his sums wrong. And usually Mrs Hatch told him to slow down and take more care with his work.

Ganesh was the same with everything he did, he always wanted to be first. He would be the first to finish writing a story, only to be told to rewrite it because it was so untidy. He would be first with a painting but would get into trouble because he had more paint on himself than on his paper.

Then one day something happened that slowed him down. Ganesh loved cricket and he was delighted to be picked for the school cricket team. It was their first hard ball match of the season and Ganesh was fielding. Jonny was bowling and the batsman swung wildly at the ball as it bounced in front of him. He edged the ball and it flew off his bat towards Ganesh. It was going to Ganesh's right hand side and he dived to catch it. The speeding ball smacked into his outstretched fingers and Ganesh felt a sudden sharp pain as the ball left his hand and continued towards the boundary.

Ganesh sat on the ground holding his right hand. His index finger was at a strange angle. He had obviously broken it. It was a home match and there were plenty of parents watching, including Ganesh's father. He came running over, took one look at Ganesh's finger and said that he must go to hospital.

The next day Ganesh returned to school with his finger all strapped up. Of course he couldn't write because he was right handed. He tried writing with his left hand but all he managed was a squiggly mess. Ganesh became very frustrated because he couldn't finish anything and everything he did was really awful.

Help us to see that being first is not important. It is how well we do something that matters, not how quickly.

Poor Ganesh, how do you think he was feeling?

It was during the English lesson when Mrs Hatch had an idea. She disappeared into Mr Bell's classroom and came back with a computer on a trolley. They had one in their classroom but it wasn't working. George had knocked Mrs Hatch's

cup of coffee all over the keyboard. Ganesh brightened up when Mrs Hatch said he could write his English work on the computer.

The class had to write a poem about something they liked doing. Ganesh wanted to write about cricket. When he sat in front of the computer, staring at the blank screen, he suddenly had an idea. He would write about his broken hand, how it happened and how it felt when the ball hit his hand. He began to slowly type in the words with his left hand. It was annoying at first not being able to type quickly. Having to work slowly meant that he had time to think about his words carefully, think about how the sentences flowed and think about what he was really trying to say.

For a change he was one of the last to finish his work. But he was concentrating so much on his poem that he didn't even notice. He printed it out and took it to Mrs Hatch. She was silent as she read it and then she said, "Ganesh, this is brilliant!" She then proceeded to read it out to the whole class. Ganesh blushed with embarrassment but he was really pleased. But there was more to come for Ganesh and his poem. Mrs Hatch sent his poem to be published in the local parish magazine. They liked to publish work by the children of their local school. A journalist from the county newspaper saw it and asked if he could publish it. That really pleased Ganesh. But it was a letter he received from the editor of *Cricketer's Weekly*, a national magazine, that made him feel on top of the world. They wanted to publish his poem and even sent a photographer to the school to take a picture of him holding his injured hand.

Ganesh's hand healed quickly and it wasn't long before he was back to working fast. But now, when Mrs Hatch told him to slow down and think about his work, just like he did for his famous poem, he knew exactly what she meant!

Discussion Points
1. Why do you think Ganesh always wanted to be first with his work?
2. Why was Ganesh so successful with his poem?
3. What lesson did Ganesh learn?

Prayer/Reflection
Dear Lord, help us to tackle our work with care and enthusiasm. Give us the inspiration to do our best, to use our talents to produce good quality work. Teach us to praise those who do their best.

Follow-up Activity
What jobs need to be done carefully? Discuss different professions in which it would be dangerous for people to rush their work. What would be the consequences of these people making mistakes? Let children draw a poster to show these professions at work, in pairs or groups.

6
The Bonfire

THEME: taking care at bonfire time; peer group pressure

Jonny, Ganesh and George stood looking at the huge stack of wood ready to be burned. The boys were in Jonny's back garden after school. Jonny wanted to show the other two the large amount of wood that he and his Dad had collected. It was bonfire night that evening and Jonny couldn't wait to set it alight and see the fireworks.

"Can you two come around tonight?" he asked as he casually threw a ball across the grass for Bess. His pet Collie dashed eagerly after the ball.

"Yea, that would be great," enthused Ganesh, "I'll have to ask my parents first but I'm sure that it'll be alright."

George looked crestfallen. He'd never been to a proper bonfire and fireworks. He lived with his mother and little brother. George always had to look after his brother on Friday evenings when his mother went out to work on a Friday evening so she would not be able to take him to Johnny's

"What about you George?" asked Jonny.

"Na, I wouldn't be allowed," replied George. He looked longingly at the pile of wood. Bess dropped her ball at Ganesh's feet and wagged her tail, waiting for him to throw the ball. Ganesh picked it up and hurled it across the garden. Bess darted off chasing the ball and disappeared behind the wood pile.

"What about lighting it now?" asked George.

"You've got to be joking," said Jonny, "my Dad would murder me."

"Just a little bit," encouraged George. "Here, look," George went up to the stack of wood and pulled a few pieces off. He then made a little heap out of twigs, dried leaves and other bits of wood. Ganesh thought it was a great idea and helped him. Jonny wasn't too sure, though.

Jonny is being put under pressure by George to do something he doesn't want to do. How should he explain this to George?

"There you are," announced George, "it's only a little stack. It'll be burnt out

Sometimes our friends can encourage us to do things that we know are wrong. Help us to be strong and to do what we know to be right.

before you know it."

"But my Dad will see where we had a fire," argued Jonny.

"I know, when it finishes we'll cover over the ashes with some damp leaves," suggested Ganesh.

"Anyway, it'll be dark when your Dad lights that lot, he'll never see this," urged George.

Jonny was convinced. After all it was only going to be a little bonfire. He raced into the house and looked through some kitchen drawers for a box of matches. His mother wasn't home from work yet so he didn't need to worry about being caught by her. He found the matches and ran back outside. The other two had made a little pile of dried leaves just under the wood to help start the fire. Jonny bent over and lit a match. It instantly blew out because of the breeze that was blowing. George and Ganesh crowded around Jonny to protect him from the

wind and he then struck another match. This time it stayed alight and he put it down to the dried leaves. The leaves instantly caught fire and flames began to lick around the twigs and then the larger sticks. The boys stood back and watched, mesmerised by the dancing flames and warmed by their glow.

Suddenly the breeze strengthened and a flash of flames shot across from the small fire to the main large stack of wood. And just as quickly that pile began to burn. The boys stood there horrified. There was nothing they could do. They stood back watching. George was thrilled, Ganesh was a little worried, but Jonny was distraught. He didn't know how he was going to face his parents.

Jonny was woken from his nightmare by the crying shrieks of a frightened animal.

"Bess!" he shouted. He ran around to the other side of the stack, a side that was only smouldering and hadn't quite caught fire. There was Bess trapped amongst the wood. Unbeknown to the boys, Bess had smelt a hedgehog which had crawled under the stack to go to sleep. Bess was now so frightened that she was panicking and found herself lost in the stack. Smoke was getting into her lungs, sparks were burning her skin and the heat from the fire was beginning to singe her fur. Then she heard Jonny calling. She turned in the direction of his voice and staggered through the branches. Suddenly she burst into the open air and was instantly swept off her feet by Jonny who carried her into the house.

Bess was fortunate. When Jonny's mother got home they rushed Bess to the vet. He checked her over and pronounced her fit. She would have a few bald patches for a while until the burnt fur grew back. She would always be terrified of fire. Less fortunate was the hedgehog. It was never seen again.

Discussion Points

1. How do you think Jonny will explain this to his parents?
2. What will his parents' reaction be?
3. Do you think Jonny should be punished?
4. What is the 'Fireworks Code'?
5. What do you think about the £5000 fine for setting off fireworks in the street?

Prayer/Reflection

Let us sit quietly and think about the dangers of bonfires and fireworks. Lord, help us to be responsible to our pets and all our friends and parents, and to be sensible and safe.

Follow-up Activities

1. Ask the children to design a Fireworks Code poster, especially featuring the care we must take with our pets.
2. This story could be acted out. Use musical instruments for the sound effects of the bonfire.

7
Who Gets the Main Part?

SITUATIONS

THEME: accepting disappointment; being fair

Delphine couldn't believe her ears. Mr Bell announced that she had been given the main part in the play. She was going to be Peter Pan! She had dreamed of the part for weeks and it had come down to deciding between herself and Rafi. The final audition was that morning and they had to sing some of the songs. They both did really well and Delphine wasn't at all confident that she was going to get the part. But she did! She felt wonderful!

"Well done, Delphine," said Rafi. She had walked over to Delphine and was standing in front of her. Disappointment was written all over Rafi's face. "I'm glad you got the part, you're a much better singer than me."

Delphine was very relieved to hear Rafi say that. Rafi was her best friend and she knew that Rafi really wanted the part of Peter Pan as well. "What part did you get?" asked Delphine.

"I'm Captain Hook's first mate," replied Rafi.

"That's a funny part, you'll enjoy that," said Delphine encouragingly.

Rafi thought for a second, "I suppose so, but I don't get to sing any solos like you."

"But it's still one of the main parts, you'll be really good at it," said Delphine. The two friends wandered back to their class, one grinning and ecstatic and the other solemn and thoughtful.

The rehearsals went well for a few weeks but then suddenly disaster struck. Delphine woke up one morning with a really sore throat and a temperature. She was coming down with the flu! She was desperate to go to school but her mother said not to be so silly, she would be away for days. It was only ten days before the show, so Delphine felt she had to go in for rehearsals. But when she secretly tried to get up she suddenly went weak and had to climb back into bed.

At school Mr Bell was worried. He had to practise the play without the main character. They tried for a few days but it was very difficult. The other children were getting their lines wrong and the singing wasn't right. Then he had an idea, "Rafi, come here."

Rafi trotted over to him, "Yes Mr Bell?"

"Look, Delphine is still away and we aren't quite sure when she'll be back. Do you think you could take over her part until she is fit?"

"Who would do my part?" asked Rafi.

"I think Clare or Ganesh could do it. They're pirates already so I'm sure they know the routine by now."

Rafi was delighted to get the chance to be Peter Pan. She loved singing and she had the opportunity to sing some very nice songs. She had been disappointed with her audition. She had just got over a cold and she couldn't quite reach the high notes as well as Delphine. Now she was a hundred percent fit she was longing to have a go.

Rafi threw herself into the rehearsal. Even though she had to sing from the script it was obvious to all that she was a better singer than Delphine. At going home time a number of children came up to her to tell her she'd done well.

By the end of the week Rafi had worked really hard and had learned the words so well that she didn't need a script. Meanwhile, life for Delphine was very frustrating. Her temperature refused to go down so after a couple of days her mother called the doctor out. He said that Delphine had an infection and prescribed an antibiotic. Unfortunately for Delphine, he also said she must stay home for at least two or three days more. Delphine felt that the whole world was against her. Was she ever going to get back to school?

Two days before the show Delphine had a big argument with her mother. Delphine's mother wanted her to stay home one more day to make sure she was fit, but Delphine insisted that she was ready to go back that morning. They decided to compromise and Delphine was allowed to return for the afternoon. Delphine didn't mind this because the rehearsals were always in the afternoon.

"Oh come on, Mum," shouted Delphine. She was waiting by her front door. Her mother was looking for her car keys. "We could have walked to school by now. They'll be starting any minute."

"All right, all right, I'm not letting you walk in the cold air and if you won't be quiet we'll not go at all," her mother said sternly. Her mother finally found her keys in another coat pocket. Delphine was by the car in a flash, silently urging her mother to hurry up. Eventually they arrived.

The ten-minute car journey seemed to take hours. The car had barely stopped when Delphine jumped out and raced into school. She first looked into her classroom but the class wasn't there. They must have already gone into the hall. She walked down the corridor towards the hall. She could hear singing, and it was one of her songs! She pushed the door open and stood there, mouth open, totally stunned. Rafi was standing on the stage, surrounded by other members of the cast. She was singing Delphine's favourite song. She was singing it beautifully and Delphine's heart sank. She knew that Rafi had taken over her part in the play and was doing it better than her.

"Delphine, how nice to see you. Are you better?" greeted Mr Bell. Everyone looked across the hall as Delphine slowly walked in. Rafi stood rooted to the spot. She had assumed that Delphine would not be back in time for the show. She started wishing that Delphine would be taken ill again and not come back. Then she felt terrible, as, after all, Delphine was her friend.

Rafi jumped off the stage and walked over to Delphine. "We've missed you, are you feeling better?" she asked.

Delphine didn't hear her, she looked at Mr Bell and asked with tears in her eyes, "Am I still Peter Pan?"

This is a dreadful situation. Should Mr Bell honour his first decision and let Delphine take the part? Yet Rafi had worked hard to learn the part and was better than Delphine. Also he didn't want to destroy the girls' friendship.

Discussion Points
1. What should Mr Bell do and how should the girls respond?
2. Describe how Delphine felt when she saw Rafi doing her part in the play.
3. Describe other times in our lives when we have to face disappointment.

The story ended quite well. Mr Bell had planned to perform the show on two evenings so the girls shared being the star. Delphine took the main part on Wednesday evening and all her family came that night. Rafi took over on Thursday night when her family came to watch. The girls had fun practising the songs together and their friendship grew even deeper.

When we want something badly, it is hard to think of others. Help us always to be fair.

Prayer/Reflection
Dear Lord, be with us through difficult times: when we are faced with illness; when we are shattered by disappointment; when our friends seem to turn against us; when we do not understand what is happening around us.
Reassure us with your presence and let us remember that where you are no ill can come.

Follow-up Activities
1. There are many times when it is difficult for a teacher to be fair. Discuss this and look at the following situations:
   • when choosing a football team should they choose just the best players or should they try to give everybody a game?
   • when two children argue over the ownership of an a pen;
   • trying to sort out who started a fight.
   Groups could devise short plays to show how they came to decisions about these situations.
2. Children could suggest situations in which parents might find it difficult to be fair. These could be discussed and then acted out in groups.

The Stranger by the Gate 8

SITUATIONS

THEME: valuing elderly people

Mrs Sidikki looked at the stranger by the gate. She remembered that he had been there that morning when she had brought Ganesh to school. The man had only stayed there a few minutes, then wandered off. He didn't appear to be with a child. In fact he was far too old to have a child in primary school. He seemed more like a grandfather. As Mrs Sidikki walked across the playground she kept looking back at the stranger. She would watch to see if he was waiting for anybody in particular. Perhaps he was a grandparent looking after his grandchildren. But what if he wasn't?

Ganesh came out of the door along with Jonny. He said hello to his mum but didn't walk with her. He felt he was much too old to walk with his mum now so he walked on ahead of her. Mrs Sidikki could hardly keep up with the boys as they all strolled across the playground towards the gate. The man was still there.

"Ganesh, wait for me," said Mrs Sidikki sternly. Ganesh stopped and looked around. He was quite surprised because it was unusual for his mother to speak to him like that at school. Mrs Sidikki caught up with Ganesh and Jonny and then deliberately stayed close to them as they walked up to the gate. When they walked through the gate she stared at the stranger. He looked at her and then immediately looked down, embarrassed, and began to shuffle down the road with his head down.

"Do you know that man? "asked Ganesh. He noticed the look that his mother gave the stranger.

"No," she replied, "and I don't like the look of him. He looks far too shifty for my liking. If I see him again I shall go into school and tell Mr Hall." And the next morning that is exactly what she did.

He was there again, looking soulfully into the playground. This time more parents began to notice and Mrs Sidikki didn't need much pushing to go straight to Mr Hall.

"You say he's been there the last few days?" he asked her.

He shouldn't be standing there watching the children

"Yes, and I don't like the look of him," she added, "I think he's dirty."

"Well thank you for telling me, I'll go and see to him right now," said Mr Hall. He left his office and went outside. He saw the stranger by the gate and walked up to him. At first Mr Hall felt a little apprehensive and wondered whether he should have called the police first. But when he got closer to the man he realised he needn't have worried. The man was very elderly, looking at least eighty and very frail. A strong wind could have blown him over. Close up he certainly didn't look threatening. His clothes, though clean, were very crumpled and his face looked thin and haggard.

"Hello, can I help you?" Mr Hall asked the stranger.

The stranger looked at Mr Hall and then at the group of parents behind him, whispering to each other. "I didn't mean to frighten anybody, I just wanted to see where Mary worked," said the old man.

"Mary?" asked Mr Hall.

"My late wife. She died recently and I found these the other day." He pulled out some old cards that said 'Good-bye' and 'Sorry You're Leaving' on them. "She used to be a helper at lunch time you know. She used to love the children."

"I know who you are," said a parent from behind Mr Hall. She came forward. It was Mrs White, Clare's mother. "You're Mary Allen's husband aren't you?" Mrs White turned to Mr Hall who was looking a little puzzled. "Mary used to be a dinner lady, before your time Mr Hall. She was a lovely person. My eldest, Helen, cried when she heard she had died a few months back. You must be Burt. She used to talk about you."

As we live and learn, we ask you to watch over us and keep us safe,

Burt's face came alive. He couldn't believe someone could have remembered all of this. "She used to love the children," said Burt. "Even when she retired she always used to talk about the children. She often said that she would have liked to come into school and help the teachers, with reading or something like that. But it was her arthritis, you know, that's why she couldn't come up."

Mr Hall felt very sorry for Burt. It was almost as if the elderly man was apologising for his wife. Burt continued, "With Mary gone I seem to have a lot of time on my hands. I've been thinking about coming in to see you but I didn't think you would want an old man like me around."

"Good heavens," replied Mr Hall, "we welcome anybody who wants to help, no matter what their age."

"I couldn't help with football, not at my age. I'm eighty-two you know," said Burt.

"Why Burt, I bet you'd be a right dazzler in your football shorts!" said Mrs White and all the parents laughed.

"We're always looking for help to hear children read," suggested Mr Hall.

"I know Mrs Hatch was asking only the other day for helpers," suggested Mrs Sidikki.

"There you are then, Burt, Mary will be proud of you," said Mrs White.

From then on Burt came up to school regularly, twice a week, to help hear children read. He became one of the most popular helpers in the school. He would sometimes bring a tape-recorder and record the children reading and play it back to them. He loved to play the tape at home to his friends. He was very proud to help at school. He was no longer the stranger at the gate but a friend welcomed in the school.

Discussion Points
1. Why was Burt reluctant to go into the school in the first place?
2. Why was Mrs Sidikki suspicious of the old man at the gate?
3. Why do the children like going to Burt to read to him?

Prayer/Reflection
Let us sit quietly and think of someone who is elderly. They might be a grandparent or a neighbour. Let us think about their feelings, whether they are lonely and need company. Let us think of their wisdom that we may learn from their rich lives. Let us value the contribution they can make to our lives.

Follow-up Activity
Elderly people love to receive letters. Ask children to think of an elderly person they know and write to them. She or he might be a neighbour or a relative. Before the children start, they can work with a partner and make a list of all the things to tell the elderly person about.

9
The Football Posts

THEME: vandalism

George liked to think he was good at football but he wasn't as good as most of the other boys. As soon as he got the ball he tended to kick it in whatever direction he was facing, even if that was towards his own goal! He was, though, fearless in the tackle. He loved sliding into a tackle, taking both the ball and his opponent's legs. But Mr Bell didn't often choose George for the team. He once muttered about George being a liability to the team. George went to all the practices and waited with anticipation to hear if he had been chosen for the team but he was usually disappointed. The team had so far played six matches and George had managed to be a substitute once. He had played for ten minutes but during that time he gave away three penalties and scored an own goal!

One evening George was at the recreation ground with his friends Rufus and Dave. They were neighbours of George and were at the secondary school. The two older boys made George go in goal and were firing shots at him. George was quite enjoying himself, he loved diving about and getting muddy. He was actually stopping quite a few shots and was beginning to wonder if goal keeper would be his best position on the team.

It was getting dark so the boys decided to kick just a couple more shots and then go home. Dave shot wide and while he went running off to retrieve the ball George glanced up at the cross bar of the goal post. George had grown a lot over the last year and was quite proud that he could now reach the cross bar. He jumped up and grabbed the bar and hung there, arms stretched. Suddenly there was a cracking sound and George quickly let go. The bar was wooden and it was obviously giving way under his weight. He then had an idea. He called the other two boys over to him and then jumped up and grabbed the cross bar again. The bar cracked more as he began to bounce up and down.

Rufus and Dave saw what he was doing and also jumped up and grabbed the bar. With their bodies twisting and turning and legs kicking wildly the cross bar eventually gave way. The laughing boys tumbled to the ground. When they got up they looked at the broken goal post, with its cross bar in two pieces. They began to look around furtively to see if anybody had seen them but it was then quite dark and nobody else was around. They started to giggle and then decided they had better get home.

Help us to think before we act & realise that our actions can end up causing harm

What are the consequences of the boys breaking the goal post?

George woke up the next morning feeling unhappy about the evening before. He was beginning to worry if somebody had seen them. The goal post was only a piece of wood, it could be easily fixed. Anyway, it wasn't all his fault, it wouldn't have broken if the others hadn't joined him. Throughout breakfast and on the way to school George kept going over in his mind what had happened. By the time he got to school he had convinced himself that it wasn't his fault and that nobody would care anyway.

"Hey, George, guess what?" shouted an excited Ganesh as he ran up to George. "You're in the football team tonight!"

"Me? Why? How come?" George couldn't believe it.

"Jonny has the flu. He's not at school today," explained Ganesh. "Mr Bell said he wanted to see the team at lunch time."

George couldn't wait. He wondered what position he was going to play in. After lunch Mr Bell gathered the team together and explained, "As you know, boys, our goal keeper, Jonny, is away. I am thinking about trying George in goal. What do you think George?"

"I'll give it a go," replied an enthusiastic George.

"If you and some of the others change now you can have a short practice."

The boys practised for fifteen minutes and it was obvious that George would be a good replacement for Jonny. What he lacked in skill he made up for in bravery when diving at attackers' feet.

The afternoon seemed to go very slowly for George. He couldn't wait until after school. At one point he looked worriedly outside when it began to pour with rain. After school the boys gathered in Mr Bell's classroom to collect their kit.

"You'll all be pleased to hear that the game will not be cancelled because

of the rain," he announced. The boys gave a hearty cheer, George being the loudest. "We do have a problem, though. Our pitch has become waterlogged so we shall have to go down to 'the rec' to play our game." The boys didn't mind that because the pitch at 'the rec' was more level than their own and it was only a ten minute walk away.

When they got there Mr Bell was having a serious talk with the teacher from the other school. Their opponents' teacher then gathered up his team and led them back to their minibus and drove away! Mr Bell came over to the puzzled boys.

"I'm afraid the game is cancelled after all," he announced.

"Why," asked Ganesh, "is the pitch too wet?"

"No, the pitch is fine, but come and have a look at this." They were standing in the car park and the changing rooms blocked their view of the football pitch. They walked around the changing rooms and then they all stood there with mouths open. "Look at what some stupid vandals did to the goal posts!" said Mr Bell, pointing to the broken cross bar. George could feel his face and ears burn. He was hoping nobody could see him. He had almost convinced himself that the night before was a dream but his stupidity was there for all to see.

The boys began to mutter words which cut George like a knife. Comments such as "stupid vandals," "selfish pigs", and "I'd like to get hold of who ever did that and break them in two," pierced his heart.

Ganesh turned to George, saying, "Tough luck, George. Jonny will probably be back for the next match." George was devastated. He had missed his chance because of his own stupid actions.

Discussion Points

1. Someone always suffers when there is an act of vandalism. Who suffered in this story? Who suffered the most?
2. Why did George break the cross bar in the first place?
3. How does George feel about his actions? What should he do next?

Prayer/Reflection

Dear Lord, help us to realise that our actions usually affect other people. Teach us to think before we act, so that we do things for the good of others, not to make them sad.

Follow-up Activity

The children can imagine they are reporters investigating an act of vandalism. If you are lucky to be in a school which has little or no vandalism then use the story above. The children can describe exactly what the vandalism is, where and how it happened. But most important, they need to write about the consequences of the vandalism, who it affects and how. The work could be in the form of a newspaper article or presented in an assembly.

10
Sticks and Stones

THEME: name calling

Clare was very upset. She knew she shouldn't have gone to school that morning, she just knew it. Her mum had said it would be alright, that nobody would say anything. But her mum didn't know George like Clare knew him. George had taken one look at her, laughed and soon the name calling started.

Clare's problem began when she had to go to the orthodontist. Her front teeth stood out slightly because she had continuously sucked her thumb when she was younger. Now she had to wear a brace in order to push her front teeth back. At first the brace felt very awkward. Clare didn't want to smile or speak. She didn't even want to open her mouth to eat! She had her brace fitted at the beginning of the half term holiday. By the weekend she was getting used to it but then it was school again and she had to face her friends.

Her best friends, Delphine and Rafi, were very kind to her. They wanted to know how it felt, did it hurt, did food get stuck behind it and how long did she have to wear it? Clare began to feel comfortable about her brace, but then George heard about it.

"What's that in your mouth?" asked an inquisitive George.

Clare didn't say anything but Rafi rounded on George, "Mind your own business, George."

"You've got train-tracks in your mouth, haven't you!" shouted George. Clare went red in the face and before Clare's friends could say anything George ran off laughing. Tears welled up in Clare's eyes.

"Ignore him," suggested Delphine, "he's just an idiot." But the damage was done. She could see George telling some of the other children in the class about her brace. Jonny walked by and said, "Hi, train-track mouth!" Clare would have turned around and walked straight out of school if Delphine and Rafi hadn't been there to comfort her.

Delphine went up to Jonny and looked him straight in the eye and said, "That was a horrible and nasty thing to say and if you dare say it again we'll tell Mrs Hatch."

Jonny looked down embarrassed. "It was George who started it," he said, pleading his excuses and turning away.

"Come on," said Delphine to Clare, "just ignore him."

The class settled into their normal morning routine and Clare was able to forget her brace and concentrate on her work. But when they went out at break time George wandered by Clare and muttered very quietly so that nobody could hear, "Train-track mouth." Clare became upset again and Delphine and Rafi were furious with George. They went to Mr Bell, who was on playground duty, and told him what George had said. Mr Bell simply advised them to ignore George, which was easier said than done. But then something happened which dramatically changed the situation.

After teasing Clare, George wondered off to join in with the other boys playing football. The ball came in his direction. He ran after it trying to get to it before Ganesh, but he was so concentrated on looking at the ball that he ran straight into Melanie Parkins. Melanie was minding her own business walking across the playground when George hurtled into her from behind. George's face smacked into the back of Melanie's head and both went sprawling onto the ground. The other children called Mr Bell who rushed over. He found Melanie sitting up holding the back of her head and crying. George was sitting holding his mouth looking very stunned. Blood began to seep through his fingers and drip over his trousers. Mr Bell led both children into school and handed them over to Mrs Hatch who dealt with the first aid. She checked both children over. Melanie had a small bump on the back of her head and was suffering from shock. George's front teeth had cut into his upper lip which was now swelling up. By the time George was cleaned up it was the end of break time and he went straight back into class.

George was feeling very sorry for himself because his whole mouth throbbed, especially his upper lip. Not many children in the class felt sorry for George because most, at some time in the past, had been bullied by him. Delphine, Rafi and Clare saw this as an opportunity to teach George a lesson.

What do you think they are going to do?

At lunch time the girls sidled up to George. He was still looking miserable with his swollen lip. "You've got a pretty face, George," remarked Delphine. George looked at her wondering what she was getting at. "What should we call you?" she continued.

"I know, how about Blobby Mouth, you know, like Mr Blobby on TV?" suggested Rafi.

George now knew what was happening and he didn't like it one bit! "Push off," he said, "I'll tell Mr Bell."

"Blobby Mouth, Blobby Mouth," the girls chanted after him as he walked away.

George went up to Mr Bell to complain that the girls were being horrible to him. He was hoping he would stop them but he was rather surprised by Mr Bell's attitude.

"Well George, everyone in the class complains about you calling them names. Now that you know what it feels like perhaps you will stop being horrible to everyone else."

George understood what Mr Bell meant and he did make an effort to stop calling the others names. A few weeks later, when his mouth was better, he teased Clare again, saying she talked as if she had cotton wool in her mouth. But instead of being upset, Clare retorted back that at least she wasn't called a Blobby Mouth. George left her alone after that.

Discussion Points
1. What lessons did George and Clare learn?
2. How can friends help someone who is being bullied?
3. How does it feel to be called horrible names?

Prayer/Reflection
Dear Lord, help us to understand the feelings of others and how they can be hurt by teasing and name calling. Help us to see when our friends are frightened or upset so that we can comfort them.

Follow-up Activity
In groups the children could make a list of different ways of dealing with verbal bullying. They could then choose one and make up a short play that could be shown to the rest of the class.

11
The Newspaper

THEME: commitment

The class sat expectantly, waiting to see who was chosen as the 'team' to produce the newspaper. Mrs Hatch had asked for volunteers and was surprised to find that half the class had put their hands up. She had planned that the class would produce a newspaper as part of the term's project on 'Communications'. All of the class would contribute but she needed an editorial team to put the paper together. She told the class that it would mean a lot of extra work, especially at lunch times. But they still wanted to do it.

She had made her decision and was now going to tell the class. "Well, I've thought about it and I have decided that Jonny should be the sports editor; Delphine to do birthdays; Ganesh the joke page; George do class trips and other special events; Clare, interviews with any visitors to the school and Rafi advertising." There was a mixture of cheers and groans as the editorial team was chosen. Mrs Hatch continued, "I would like to see you six at playtime this morning to discuss your jobs."

The six children gathered around excitedly, saying well done to each other. During the morning break Mrs Hatch outlined their jobs and how the newspaper was going to be put together. A lot of extra time was going to be needed for working on the computers at lunch times in order to finish the paper by the end of the term. The children all agreed that they would be committed to the project. Unfortunately, one of them was going to let the others down.

The project started well enough. The children put in the extra work on the computers and articles, features and advertisements began to be produced. They harried and badgered the other children in the class to produce work for them to type into the computers. After a few weeks the file of finished work began to grow.

One lunch time Mrs Hatch was having a look through the finished articles when she noticed that there were some missing. "Rafi, who was supposed to be organising the sports reports?"

Rafi was at one computer designing an advert, "It's Jonny, Miss," she replied.

Dear Lord, We know that we should only make promises that we know we can keep. Help us to be sensible in the promises & commitments that we make.

"Well, there's only one report here and yet there have been quite a few football and netball matches, not to mention the chess league and last week's gym competition. Where is Jonny?" she asked, casting an eye around the classroom and realising that Jonny was the only one of the team not there.

"I think he's outside playing football," said Ganesh.

"Oh, is he," said Mrs Hatch as she walked to the door. She went out to the playground and spotted Jonny playing with a group of boys. She called Jonny and he ran over looking rather sheepish. "Jonny, where are the sports reports for the newspaper?" she asked.

"I'm working on them, ~~Miss~~ *Mrs. Hatch*," replied Jonny. "I've left some at home and some of the others in the class haven't given me their reports to type up."

"I suggest you bring the ones you're working on to school tomorrow and you had better start chasing the children who owe you the other reports."

The next day Mrs Hatch made sure that some of the other children writing sports reports managed to find time to type up their reports onto the computer. But Jonny still didn't arrive at lunch time to meet up with the other members of the team. They were now beginning to put the pages of the newspaper together, that is, all the pages except the sports pages. When Mrs Hatch had told Jonny he was needed at lunch time in order to start putting his sports pages together he had promised he would be there. But he didn't turn up.

Jonny has broken his promise, what should Mrs Hatch do?

"This is ridiculous," said a very annoyed Mrs Hatch. "The paper should be finished by now, where is that boy?"

You knew this would be a big commitment Jonny & you were keen to be on the editorial team. You must play your part if the Newspaper is to succeed

"We can do the sports page," suggested Ganesh with George beside him. "We've got most of the reports from the others. Rafi is going to finish the article about the gym festival. We can then put the whole page together."

"Go ahead then," replied Mrs Hatch, "I'm sure you will do just as good a job as Jonny."

And they did. They worked very hard during the next few lunch times and after school. There was no sign of Jonny. He was always outside playing football. When they finished the newspaper Mrs Hatch proudly presented it to the rest of the class. All the children contributed to the newspaper but the editors put it together.

"And I've got a surprise for you all," announced Mrs Hatch, "I've arranged a visit to the local newspaper, the *Daily Gazette*, next week. While we are there I thought it would be nice for our editorial team to have their photograph taken with Mr Bloomer, the editor of the *Gazette*."

"Which day will the picture be published?" asked Jonny. "I want to make sure my Mum buys the paper with my picture in it."

"That's not fair," said Ganesh, "you didn't do anything."

"I was chosen to be on the editorial team," argued Jonny.

"Ganesh is right," said Mrs Hatch. "Though you were on the team you let them down. You were too busy playing football and you forgot to turn up. Ganesh and George did all your work so I don't think you should be in the picture."

Discussion Points

1. Was Mrs Hatch right to exclude Jonny from the picture?
2. If Jonny was not prepared to fulfil his commitment then what should he have done?
3. Discuss the concept of 'commitment', especially when people volunteer to help others. What would happen if volunteer helpers with the Red Cross or RNLI decided not to fulfil their commitments?

Prayer/Reflection

Dear Lord, help us to think of others and how we can help them instead of just thinking about ourselves. Help us to think not of how much we can get out of life but how much we can put into life. Help us to keep our promises and not to let others down.

Follow-up Activity

In pairs ask the children to make two lists: list A, promises that are sensible and easy to keep, e.g. making their bed before coming to school; and list B, promises that would be impossible to keep, e.g. writing a ten page letter to their grandmother every day. Are there any other kinds of promises which are difficult but possible?

12
The School Trip

THEME: listening to instructions

The children always enjoyed a day out from normal school. On this occasion they were going to the museum to look at the Roman exhibition. Before lunch they were going to have a guided tour and a talk with slides. After lunch they would have worksheets to do. But for Clare the highlight was going to be visiting the shop. Her Gran had given her £5 the day before and it was burning a hole in her pocket, just waiting to be spent.

When the class arrived they were greeted by two museum guides. Mrs Hatch divided the class into two groups, one to go with each guide. They put their lunch in the canteen and while one group did the tour the other had the slide show. They then swapped around after an hour. The children found the exhibition fascinating. They saw examples of Roman mosaics and other art, models of houses and towns. Their favourite section showed clothes, jewellery and armour.

Lunch time came very quickly. Clare sat with Rafi and Delphine. "What are you going to buy in the shop?" she asked them.

"I've only got fifty pence so I'll get a postcard or a pencil," answered Delphine.

"I'm saving my money," said Rafi. "My Mum is picking me up at three thirty, as soon as we get back to school. We've got to catch a train to Birmingham because it is my grandparents wedding anniversary. My Mum said I might be able to spend some money at the station."

After lunch Mrs Hatch called the class together. "Now children, listen very carefully. We've got an hour and a half before the bus leaves to take us back to school. In order to get back by three thirty we must meet here at three o'clock. Now did you all listen? I want you back here by ... what time Jonny?"

"Three o'clock, Miss."

"Well done, I'm glad you're listening, I hope everyone else is as well. The worksheets should take you about an hour to finish, that will give you thirty minutes to look at anything else in the exhibition and visit the shop. Now remember what I said before we left school, you must be on your best behaviour, no running or shouting. Now go with your partner and finish your worksheets."

Clare wanted to work with Rafi and Delphine but they weren't allowed to go in threes so she was paired up with Julia. The two girls decided to do the section on houses first. They made observational drawings and looked for answers to the written questions. Then they wandered off to work on the sections about clothes.

After an hour Clare couldn't wait any longer. She turned to Julia and said, "Come on, we've done enough, let's go to the shop." The two girls put their pencils away and went to the museum shop. Quite a few other children were there already.

Clare looked around the shop. There was quite an array of things to buy: pencils, erasers, postcards, notelets, mugs, purses, pretend Roman jewellery and pottery, and lots more. She spent so much time deciding whether to buy a red purse or a blue one that she didn't notice the others slowly drifting away. She chose the blue purse and then spotted some pretend stick-on earrings. She looked at her watch. There was plenty of time so she spent the next ten minutes deciding which pair of earrings to buy.

Meanwhile, back at the canteen, Mrs Hatch was counting the children. There was one missing. "Who hasn't got their partner?" she asked the class.

"Me, Miss, Clare's not back," called Julia.

"Right then, it's three o'clock and we need to get going." Mrs Hatch turned to her classroom assistant, "Mrs Holden, will you please see the class onto the coach, I'll find Clare."

Mrs Hatch first went to the shop but was surprised to find Clare was not there. In fact she was there but at that moment she had bent down behind a book case to look at some Roman mosaic style bookmarks. Mrs Hatch hastily looked around, didn't see Clare and went out again. She then checked the toilets and, not finding Clare there, she went into the exhibition rooms. For fifteen minutes she searched. She was now beginning to feel quite panicky. She reached the canteen again and looked at her watch. It was three twenty. They were going to be very

late back to school. It was at that moment that Clare sauntered into the room, without an obvious care in the world, until she heard Mrs Hatch's voice.

"Where have you been, didn't you know what time you had to be back here?"

Clare looked puzzled, she thought she was early! "Three thirty?" she whispered, knowing that it was the wrong answer.

"No! You didn't listen, I asked you all to be back by three o'clock. We have to be back to school by three thirty and we're going to be late now because of you. Come on, quickly now, let's get to the bus."

Clare nearly had to run to keep up with Mrs Hatch. When they got onto the bus all the other children gave a sarcastic cheer and clap. Clare sat down beside Julia, very red in the face and trying not to look at anybody.

The bus didn't arrive back at school until four o'clock. All the parents were waiting at the school gate. Clare could see some of them looking at their watches. As soon as Rafi got off the bus her mother rushed up and pulled her away. As they walked quickly away from the bus Clare could hear Mrs Chadda's voice, "Why are you so late? I knew you shouldn't have gone on that trip. We're going to miss the train now and there won't be another one for another hour."

"It wasn't my fault," pleaded Rafi and she managed to give Clare a withering look before she walked out of sight.

Mrs Hatch stood by Clare, "Oh dear, it looks like you have ruined somebody's evening out."

With tears in her eyes all Clare could do was murmur, "Sorry."

Discussion Points
1. What does 'burning a hole in your pocket' mean?
2. Why was it important for all the children to listen to Mrs Hatch?
3. What do you think Clare was thinking about instead of listening?
4. What were the consequences of Clare not listening?

Prayer/Reflection
Dear Lord, thank you for the gift of hearing. Help us to use this gift to listen to others when they speak to us.

Follow-up Activities
1. Ask the children to describe the sounds that help them to concentrate and then to describe the sounds that they find distracting.
2. In pairs the children are given a number of topics to discuss, such as their favourite sport or television programme. Then ask each in turn to describe what their partner said.
3. In small groups, one child is given a picture which the others cannot see. This child must describe the picture for the other children in the group to draw.

13

The Promise

THEME: fulfilling promises

I t was the weekend at last and Delphine couldn't wait. Not that she was doing anything special, she was just tired out after a very busy week. She went on a school trip to the museum, she was in a netball match and she went to the after school gym club. She was now glad to do nothing. She walked through the front door, dropped her bag by the stairs, flung her coat over the banister and then flopped down onto the lounge settee. She pressed the remote control of the television and sat transfixed as *Blue Peter* came to life.

"Delphine!" called her mother from the hallway, "Come here."

"What?" asked Delphine, not moving.

"I'm not having your things littering the house. Come here and put your bag and coat away properly."

"I'll do it later," called Delphine.

Delphine was then aware of the large shape of her mother looming over her, holding her bag and coat. "Now, young lady, you're not the only one who has had a busy week."

Delphine knew when her mother meant business so she rolled off the settee and got to her feet. Without speaking she snatched her coat and bag and stomped upstairs to her room where she dumped them both onto the middle of the floor. She then flopped onto her bed and was just about to switch on her radio when the telephone downstairs rang. She heard her mother pick up the telephone and after a moment's pause she called upstairs, "Delphine, it's for you."

Delphine leapt off her bed and started to run downstairs. She thought maybe it would be Rafi or Clare to arrange something for the weekend. But when she took the telephone from her mother, she found it wasn't one of her friends on the line but her grandmother.

"Hello, Delphine, are you coming around this evening?" her grandmother asked. Delphine had promised to help her clean out a kitchen cupboard. It was high up and Delphine was going to stand on a chair and hand things down to her.

"I can't come tonight, Grandma, it's because ... I've got lots of homework to do and I've got to use a book tonight and then give it back to Rafi tomorrow."

"Okay, you must do your homework. When will you come over? I really want to clean the cupboard," asked her grandmother.

"Tomorrow, say ten o'clock, would that be alright?"

"Yes, that would be fine. I'll be waiting for you. Now give the telephone back to your mother, I want to speak with her." Delphine gave the telephone back to her mother and then went into the lounge to watch television.

A few minutes later her mother came into the lounge and turned the television off. "I was watching that," said Delphine.

"I think you had better go upstairs and get on with this homework you have to do. You obviously have *so* much to do." Her mother gave her that look that said 'I don't believe a word you're saying'.

That evening Delphine spent in her room listening to the radio. Whenever she heard her mother come upstairs she pretended to be working.

The next day was Saturday which meant that Delphine could have a lie in. In fact she had a really good lie in because it was the telephone ringing that woke her up, at eleven o'clock! She heard her father calling her, "Delphine, it's Grandma. Were you supposed to be helping her at ten o'clock?"

Delphine staggered out of bed and stood by her bedroom door, "Tell her I'll be there this afternoon, say two o'clock, I promise." She then got dressed and went downstairs.

"Your mother has gone shopping. Do you want breakfast or lunch?" asked her father.

"I'll just have a coffee and have lunch later," she replied. She got her coffee and then settled down in front of the lounge television to watch the Saturday morning programmes. She had only watched ten minutes when there was a knock on the front door. When she opened the door Rafi and Clare were standing there.

"Do you fancy coming into town, we're meeting some of the others at the Burger Bar?" asked Rafi.

"Oh yes, hang on I'll just put my shoes on," replied Delphine excitedly. She put her shoes on, grabbed her coat, made sure her purse was in her pocket and stood by the door. "Dad, I'm just popping into town with Rafi and Clare. Tell Mum I'll have something to eat out, I'll be back by tea time." She was gone before her father could reply.

What had Delphine forgotten to do? What do you think might be the consequence of this ?

It was four hours later when Delphine got home. When she walked into the house she shouted, "Mum, I'm home." But there was no answer. She searched the house but she couldn't find either of her parents. She looked around the kitchen to see if a note had been left but there was nothing. Delphine bit her lip, she felt nervous. Her parents had never left her alone like this before, at least not without a note to say where they were. The house seemed dark and lonely.

Just then the telephone rang, the noise made her jump. Delphine ran to the telephone, "Is that you Mum?" she cried down the phone. She breathed a great sigh of relief when she heard the familiar voice of her mother.

"You're home at last," her mother said, "I've been trying to get you for the last hour and a half."

"I've been with Rafi in town," replied Delphine, "didn't Dad tell you?"

"I thought you were going to be helping your grandmother," said her mother.

"Oh, I forgot, I'll go around there now," suggested Delphine.

"No, you're too late!" her mother was nearly shouting down the telephone.

"Why, what do you mean?" asked Delphine. She could tell something was wrong by the tone of her mother's voice.

"Your grandmother is in hospital. That is where we are now. She waited for you this afternoon and when you didn't arrive, *as you had promised*, she tried to clean her cupboards on her own. She climbed onto a chair, lost her balance and fell off." Delphine couldn't believe what she was hearing.

"Is she all right?" whispered Delphine.

"She has broken her collar bone and she has a nasty bump on her head. They will keep her here in hospital for a few more days just to make sure that is all that is wrong with her." There was a pause before her mother said, "Your father and I think we all need to have a good talk about keeping promises and responsibilities. Do you know what I mean?"

"Yes, I'm sorry Mum," said Delphine. She put the telephone down and then waited for them to come home.

Discussion Points
1. What was the consequence of Delphine not fulfiling her promise to her grandmother?
2. Is it fair to blame Delphine for her grandmother's accident?
3. What does Delphine need to do now?

Prayer/Reflection
Dear God, help us to give and care for others. Help us to keep the promises we make to others.

Follow-up Activity
Through making up their own short stories and role play in groups, the children can show the consequences of being let down by someone who has broken a promise.

14
SITUATIONS

Give Us Your Dinner Money!

SITUATIONS

THEME: bullying

When Jonny first started in the Juniors he had a very nasty experience. He was bullied by older children. Here is the story of what happened.

Jonny was really pleased that morning. It was to be the first time his mum allowed him to go to school on his own. Jonny had been begging his mother for some weeks for this. After all, his friends went to school on their own now. His mother finally gave in and said yes. So on Monday morning Jonny finally walked to school on his own.

When he arrived at the school gate he looked across the playground. He could see his friends, Ganesh and George, kicking a ball around at the far end. He began to run across the playground to join them when he was stopped by two older Junior boys. They were known in the playground as Mat and Stan. Mat was the leader and was a real bully, especially with younger children. Stan was just stupid, always playing up in class. Nobody ever wanted to play with either boy so they tended to stick together, wandering around the playground at break time looking for trouble. It was Mat who stopped Jonny by grabbing hold of his bag.

"Hey Squirt, where's your mummy today?" Jonny was suddenly wishing his mother was with him! He didn't reply. Mat began to search in Jonny's bag. "What have you got for lunch today? I could do with a snack."

"Leave me alone, I have school dinners," whimpered Jonny.

Mat was about to stop looking when he found Jonny's purse. "What's this then?" he announced triumphantly .

"Give it here," said an excited Stan. He took the purse from Mat, opened it and took out a £1 coin. "We've struck it lucky, we've found somebody who pays for his school dinner."

"Give it back, I need it for my lunch," cried Jonny. He looked up at the two boys and all he could see were their sneering faces. He felt he was in a bad dream and momentarily closed his eyes and opened them again. They were still there.

"You say to your teacher that you'll bring in your money tomorrow, say you forgot it today," said Stan.

"Yeah, and tomorrow you bring in £1.50. That's an extra 50p for us. Do you understand?" said Mat as he flung the bag back at Jonny. "We'll see you here tomorrow, same time. And if you don't come, you know what will happen to you?"

"N.n.n.o," stammered Jonny.

"We'll stick your head in the toilet and flush it!" gibed Stan.

"So don't tell anyone, this is our little secret," warned Mat.

We know that it is wrong to threaten people, to hurt them or to take from them. Help us to see that if we behave like that, no-one will want to be

our friend

GIVE US YOUR DINNER MONEY!

The two boys then walked off laughing, leaving Jonny standing on the spot, shaking with fright. Nobody had ever treated him like that before, he didn't know what to do. Sam and George ran up to him.

"What did they want?" asked Sam.

"They took my dinner money," blurted out Jonny who then started to cry.

The boys commiserated with Jonny. Sam had once had his crisps taken by Mat. George always went home for dinners so he had nothing to steal. All day Jonny kept a wary eye out for the two bullies. During afternoon play his worst fears looked like happening. He noticed the boys running towards him. He was about to flinch thinking they were actually going to attack him but they ran by shouting, "See you tomorrow, Squirt." Jonny was hoping that they had forgotten all about it but he was mistaken.

"Why don't you tell Mr Hall?" suggested George.

"I can't," said Jonny. "They'll stick my head down the toilet."

"They always say that," said Sam. "Have you actually heard of anybody having their head flushed in the loo?" George and Jonny looked at him, wondering what he was getting at. Sam explained, "Mr Hall once said that all bullies are cowards, they just say things to frighten people."

"What should I do?" asked Jonny.

"I've got an idea," said Sam and he set about explaining his plan.

What do you think is Ganesh's idea?

The next day Jonny walked to school feeling rather worried. What if Sam's plan didn't work? He secretly put £1.50 into his purse from his money box, just in case. When he arrived at the school gate he stopped, not wanting to go in. Mat and Stan were there, leaning against the wall, waiting for him. Jonny wanted to turn around and run back home. Then he saw Sam and his other friends and that gave him the courage to carry on.

As he walked through the gate Mat and Stan came towards him. "Well if it isn't Squirt. Where's the £1.50?" Mat demanded, holding out his hand.

"You said just 50p for you," argued Jonny.

"We've changed our minds, we want it all."

Then Jonny shouted in a loud voice, "No I won't, I'm not giving you anything." That was a signal for Sam, George, Simon and Aaron to stand behind Jonny giving support to his defiance.

"Jonny's not giving you any more money," said Sam.

"Oh yeah, did he tell you what we'll do to anybody who defies us?" warned Mat.

"You can't frighten all of us together," said George. "If you try we'll all go to Mr Hall and tell him what you're doing."

Mat and Stan looked at the five determined younger boys. "You're not worth the hassle," said Mat and then the two boys walked away.

The five boys gave a collective sigh of relief and began to do 'high fives' with each other. They were all ready to run like the wind if Mat and Stan were to get nasty but their bravado paid off. The two bullies didn't bother Jonny again except for the odd scowl and calling him Squirt whenever they walked by. But that didn't bother Jonny, he just ignored them.

That was a long time ago. Jonny and his friends are now in the top Juniors themselves. Jonny remembers how he felt when he was bullied, so whenever he sees another pupil being bullied he offers his help and support.

Discussion Points

1. Should Jonny tell his mother about the bullies? Why didn't he?
2. How did Jonny's friends help him?
3. What do you think would happen if Mat and Stan tried it again?
4. If Jonny was a pupil at our school, what would he have done?

Prayer/Reflection

We do many things together with our friends, go for walks, read a book, play with our toys. Our friends are also people to talk to, to ask for help, guidance and support when we are feeling vulnerable and frightened. We give thanks for all the wonderful friends we have.

Follow-up Activities

1. Ask each child to individually write down a few sentences describing a time when they have been bullied. After a couple of minutes put the children into groups of three or four and ask them to share their experiences. Each group can pick one of the instances of bullying written down and develop it further in terms of how the victim could have sought help from his/her friends. This could then be shown to the rest of the class as a short play.
2. Every child has the right to be free from any kind of bullying at school. Many children will say that they have been bullied but a distinction needs to be made between name calling when they are falling out with their friends and some kind of continuous abuse.

   Put the children into groups and ask them to make a list of all the types of bullying they have encountered. Teachers need to take care with this though, as a lot of bullying goes on amongst children in the same class and you may find that victim and bully are in the same group. Ask each group to report back and then choose the most common forms. Then ask the groups to work out the kinds of strategies the children need to use in order to counter the bullying. Some questions that need to be asked are:
   - What should you do when you see a friend being bullied?
   - What do you think bullying is? How is it different from other problems in friendship?
   - When should an adult be informed and who should it be?
   - How can you avoid situations that might encourage a bully?

15
Wet Playtime

THEME: behaving sensibly during wet playtimes

Everyone hated wet play times. The teachers hated them because they didn't get their coffee break in the morning. The meal time assistants hated them because the children were usually very loud and very noisy. But the children hated them worst of all because they couldn't get outside to stretch their legs and have a break from the confines of the classroom.

Delphine, Rafi and Clare were bored. They were usually allowed a netball at playtime and enjoyed practising shooting. They didn't get outside in the morning and it was still pouring with rain by lunch time. They had finished their lunch and were moping about in their classroom. The dinner ladies were patrolling the corridors, popping into each classroom, checking to make sure that the children were behaving.

Mrs Robson had come in, told Jonny and George to sit down and behave and then wandered on down the corridor. Delphine got up. She was desperate to do something. Most of the children were playing games such as *Snakes and Ladders* and *Ludo*. A group of boys were drawing pictures of racing cars from a book. Then Delphine spotted Rachel. Rachel was an extremely intelligent person who always produced lovely work. She was also the most obnoxious person in the class because she knew she was better than most of the class and was always lording it over the others. Rachel Parsons was a very unpopular girl who didn't like to mix with the other children in the class.

Hanging over Rachel's chair was her black leotard. They had enjoyed PE that morning and Rachel had not put her leotard away into her PE bag. Rachel was quietly reading a book. How she could concentrate with all the noise going on nobody knew, or cared. Delphine pretended to walk over to the book corner and as she passed Rachel she grabbed the leotard, rolled it into a ball and threw it to Clare.

"Hey, that's mine, give it back!" shouted Rachel. Delphine and Clare were joined by Rafi and the three began to throw the leotard to each other keeping it

away from Rachel. The three girls were all in the school netball team so they were good at throwing and catching. They moved easily around the room tossing the leotard high in the air just out of Rachel's reach.

After a few minutes Rafi got bored with this game. She was standing by the door when Clare threw her the leotard. She caught it, then, instead of passing it on to Delphine, she opened the door and threw it out into the corridor.

"Thank you very much!" shouted a puffing Rachel as she flounced out to retrieve her leotard.

"Quick, close the door," said Delphine, "don't let her in."

Delphine and Rafi slammed the door shut but as they did so they heard a piercing scream. Everyone in the classroom stopped what they were doing and looked towards the classroom door. Rafi opened it again and there stood Rachel with her fingers caught in the door frame. She had been trying to stop the door from being closed and her fingers had got jammed. Rachel stood there looking at her hand. Slowly, then more quickly, blood began to drip down onto the floor. The pain was so great that Rachel's face turned white and then she toppled forward into faint.

Mrs Robson was on the spot in seconds. "Quickly go to the staff room and get Mr Hall," she shouted. Ganesh and Jonny ran down the corridor to get help. Delphine, Rafi and Clare were rooted to the spot, not believing what had happened.

Later, when Rachel had been taken to hospital, Mrs Hatch, their teacher, stood in front of a silent class. "Now, who is going to start explaining exactly what happened to Rachel?" she asked the class.

Discussion Points
1. What kind of activities could the children do during wet playtimes?
2. The girls were being very unkind to Rachel. What should they do now?

Prayer/Reflection
Dear Lord, teach us always to act with kindness and truth. Help us to act sensibly so that we do not hurt others.

Follow-up Activities
1. Get three children to act being Delphine, Clare and Rafi. They are to explain in detail how the accident happened.
2. As a design and technology activity the children could make up their own games to play at wet playtimes.
3. Ask children to discuss their own activities at wet playtimes. What could be done to improve these times? Could they each write a short list of things to do, a plan, for the next wet playtime, and then try it out?

16
Manners

THEME: the importance of manners

George was a person who learned about manners the hard way. Throughout most of his years at Ford Street Primary School his manners were appalling. Here are some of the things he did.

At the end of every Friday assembly Mr Hall always gave out merit certificates. These were usually given to children who had been working hard the previous week or who had done something special.

Mrs Hatch was impressed at how well George was working and settling into her class. George had watched other children go up to Mr Hall to collect their certificates and he was surprised when his name was called. George proudly walked up to Mr Hall and tried to take the certificate from him. But Mr Hall wouldn't let the certificate go. George looked at him. Mr Hall had a serious face whilst he held onto George's certificate. George tried to take it again but Mr Hall still wouldn't let go.

"What do you say, George, when somebody gives you something?" asked Mr Hall. George stood there with mouth open not knowing what to say. "We say th......" prompted Mr Hall.

"Oh, thank you," said George finally and Mr Hall smiled and gave him his certificate. That was George's first lesson on manners.

His second lesson came the following Monday. George was busy doing his maths when he realised he had made a mistake. He looked around his table but nobody had a rubber. He went up to Mrs Hatch who was busy with some other children.

"Now Delphine, here is how you can work out the answer using a ..."

"Can I have a rubber?" interrupted George. He leaned across Delphine and looked at Mrs Hatch.

"Pardon George, do you have a problem?" she asked.

"Can I have a rubber? I made a mistake."

"George, you do not interrupt while I am speaking to someone else. Just wait, I'll sort you out in a minute."

George stood by the table waiting. When Mrs Hatch finished explaining to Delphine she asked, "Now George, what is your problem?"

"I need a rubber," explained George.

Mrs Hatch looked at him and said "I need a rubber ... "She waited expectantly for him to say the right word.

"Do you need a rubber too?" asked George.

"No, when you ask for something you should say a special word," explained Mrs Hatch. "Does anybody here know what I mean?" A number of children put their hands up. "Ganesh?"

"You should say 'please'," said Ganesh.

"Well George, what do you want?"

"Can I have a rubber ... please?" said George finally.

Mrs Hatch took a rubber from her desk and handed it to George. George took it without a word and began to walk back to his desk. "George, come back here." A puzzled looking George went back to Mrs Hatch. "What do you say when somebody gives you something?"

George thought for a moment and then remembered. "Thank you," he said. Then he was allowed to go back to his desk to carry on with his work.

George's third lesson happened a few days later. Mr Hall and Mr Bell were standing in the corridor talking about arrangements for the school concert. Mr Bell was holding an armful of music scores when a whirlwind with red hair ran between them and knocked his scores out of his hands and scattered them all over the floor.

"George, come here!" boomed Mr Hall at the departing figure of George. George stopped and walked back, surveying what he had done. "That was extremely rude of you to walk between Mr Bell and myself like that when we were talking to each other. Look what you've done!"

George went red in the face and managed to mutter "Sorry".

"I should think you are sorry. In future you either walk around people or wait until they have finished talking and then say 'excuse me' when you walk by them. Manners, George, where are your manners?"

Poor George, he had never really been told about manners. He was having to learn quickly now! George had one more lesson to learn and this time he really did remember his lesson.

His class were doing a project looking at life during the Second World War. He thought it was a great project as he was a keen aeroplane model maker. He brought in his favourite model of a World War Two Lancaster bomber. He enjoyed showing it to the rest of the class and it took pride of place on the display table. Mr Bell's class was also doing the Second World War and when he saw the model he asked George if he would like to show his class as well. George was delighted to do so and once again he stood in front of a class to talk about his model. George left his model in Mr Bell's classroom for the children to look at. Mr Bell said he would bring it back later in the day.

Help us to remember that saying please + thank you costs us no effort but it means a lot to others. Help us to be well mannered.

55

George didn't deliberately have bad manners, he just didn't know any better. When staff were going through a door usually children stood to one side to let them through and if the member of staff was carrying something then one of the children would open the door. But George couldn't be bothered about such things. So when George was going through a door in one direction and Mr Bell was coming through from another direction, and carrying a pile of books, George didn't open the door for Mr Bell. Oh no, he just barged his way through, letting the door close onto Mr Bell causing him to drop the books he was carrying.

George stopped when he heard the books fall to the ground. He had a horrible feeling that he had done something wrong again. But when he looked at the floor it wasn't the scattered books that made his heart stop. It was his model aeroplane, his best model, smashed into hundreds of pieces on the floor. Mr Bell had been carrying it back to George's class. It was perched on top of the exercise books, that is, until George had crashed his way through the door. Mr Bell was going to shout at George but he only needed to look at George's face to see that he had learned his lesson.

Discussion Points

1. Why didn't Mr Bell need to tell George off at the end?
2. What were some of the manners George had to learn?
3. Why do we need manners? What is their purpose?
4. Give examples of other times when we need good manners.

Prayer/Reflection

O lord you know what is best for our lives,
Thank you for the teaching and example of Jesus Christ.
Help us to keep on the path of goodness,
Forgive us when we stray. make mistakes
Help us to try to be polite and gracious, grateful and caring,
Always.

Follow-up Activity

Ask the children to individually write down two manners that they feel are very important. Then get the children into groups. Each group chooses the two manners that they think are the most important. When this is finished make a class list of the manners each group have chosen and discuss which are the most important. This can then lead to role play situations or creative writing.

17
A Pet Lost but a New Friend Found

THEME: having to give up something you really love

Rafi had always wanted a pet. She nagged and nagged her parents but they usually said no. They once let her have a goldfish but that only lived for a few months. Anyway, it wasn't the same as a rabbit or a guinea pig, or a cat or a dog. You can't cuddle a goldfish as well as you can cuddle a dog; in fact you can't cuddle a goldfish at all! Rafi's parents always had a reason for not having a pet. Who would feed it? Who would clean it out? Who would exercise it? Who would clean the little messes it might leave in the house? Who would pay for the vet's bills when it was ill? Rafi said she would do all these things. But it was to no avail, her parents were just as determined to say no as she was determined to keep trying.

One day during the Easter holidays she was at the recreation ground with Clare and Delphine. They were hanging around the swings just chatting about what they were going to do that evening. It was the first really lovely day that spring and they were enjoying the warmth of the sun. An ice-cream van had arrived earlier and the girls were each eating a soft ice-cream in a crunchy cone with a chocolate ripple bar stuck in the middle.

Rafi had noticed that one of the laces on her trainers had come undone so she carefully placed her half eaten ice-cream cone on the seat of the swing and bent over to tie her laces up. She stood up and turned to take her ice-cream when she exclaimed in anger, "Who's taken my ice-cream?" She looked at Clare and Delphine who were both in fits of laughter. Rafi looked to where Clare was pointing and there, dashing off with her ice-cream was a little Jack Russell dog. When he was far enough away he stopped and hungrily ate the ice-cream.

"Why didn't you stop him?" asked Rafi. She had been enjoying her ice-cream and didn't see the funny side at all.

"He was so quick, he was gone before we noticed," said Delphine, trying hard not to laugh any more.

The ice-cream was eaten in seconds and then the little dog trotted up to the girls and sat looking at Clare, waiting to see if she was going to give him a bit of hers. Rafi's anger quickly vanished as she looked at his cute face. He was predominately white in colour but with some round patches on his back and a brown patch on his face which covered one eye and ear. His mouth was open as if he was smiling.

"I think he's starving," said Rafi, who bent down to stroke him. He obviously enjoyed being stroked and wagged his little stumpy tail. First Clare and then Delphine gave him a piece of their ice-cream cone.

"He hasn't got a collar, I wonder where he comes from?" asked Rafi.

"Perhaps his owner is in 'the rec' and looking for him," suggested Clare. She stood up and looked around but didn't see anybody searching for a dog.

"I wonder what his name is," said Delphine. The girls tried a number of names but he didn't respond to any until Rafi called 'Harry' and then he leapt up and down.

"Harry? That's a stupid name to call a dog!" laughed Clare.

The girls then played with Harry, chasing him around the trees and throwing sticks, which he ran after and brought back. It was then time to go home.

"What are we going to do about Harry?" asked Clare. "We can't just leave him here."

"I'll take him home with me," said Rafi.

"Why you?" demanded Clare and Delphine together.

"Have you two forgotten, you've both got pets," explained Rafi. "I haven't any."

"What about your parents?" asked Clare.

"I think they'll be alright. It's only until we can find his owner." With that Rafi picked up Harry and took him home.

"I am not having that dog in the house!" was the reaction of Rafi's mother.

"But Mum, I'll look after him," pleaded Rafi, "it's only until we can find his owner."

"He'll ruin the new carpets," continued her mother.

"Well, what if we keep him in the garage?" suggested Rafi. "Please?"

"Alright, but only until the end of the holidays, and if you haven't found his owner then he'll have to go to the RSPCA."

Rafi was over the moon. She spent the rest of the day in the garden playing with Harry. She found some rope in the shed and tied it around his neck and pretended to walk him on a lead. That evening she tried putting him into the garage but Harry barked and then cried. He obviously didn't like being away from people. Rafi's father agreed that Harry could stay in the kitchen. Before going to bed Rafi worked at the kitchen table making notices to go into shop windows asking if anybody had lost Harry. When she tried closing the kitchen door he cried again so she quietly carried him up to her bedroom where he nestled onto the end of her bed and instantly fell asleep.

Over the next few days Rafi put notices in shops about Harry but she was hoping nobody would reply. She bought him a collar and lead so that she could take him to the recreation ground and they spent many happy hours with the other girls, playing. Even Rafi's mother and father began to enjoy Harry's company. A few times Rafi caught her father outside having a good game with Harry.

Help us to accept that we cannot always have what we want. Help us to understand the reasons why.

It was nearing the end of the holidays. Rafi was getting worried about what her mother had said about the RSPCA. She couldn't bear to have Harry locked in a small cage and then put down if nobody claimed him.

"Mum, if nobody contacts us by the end of the holidays do you think we could keep him?"

Her mother was doing the ironing and Harry was asleep by the lounge fire. She put down the iron and looked at the sleeping dog. "Well it seems as if he has decided to keep us. I suppose so. I think I'd miss him myself if we had to give him back now." Rafi threw her arms around her mother and said thank you. She was now the happiest girl in the world!

It was Sunday, the day before Rafi was due to go back to school. She was really not looking forward to going out the door on Monday morning leaving Harry behind. She was teaching him to stay and come on command when she heard the doorbell ring. She didn't take any notice, it was probably one of the neighbours. She then heard her mother calling her from the back door. When she looked around she saw her mother standing by the door and beside her was a very elderly gentleman, with white hair and bent over, supported by a stick. Suddenly Harry saw him and dashed over to him and jumped up and down with excitement.

"Rufus, you little scallywag, so this is where you've been hiding," exclaimed the old man. He was just as excited as Harry and would have jumped up and down as well if he could. The elderly man, whose name was Mr Osborn, turned to Rafi's mother and said, "Thank you so much for looking after him. He is all I have now, since my wife died a few years back. My children are living in Canada so Rufus is my family now. You have no idea how I felt when he went missing from my garden last month. He probably saw a squirrel and chased him out of the garden and then decided to go walkabout. When I saw your card at the shop I just knew it was him. How strange you called him Harry, that's my name!"

Rafi realised that she had lost Harry, or Rufus as his real name was. Tears came to her eyes as she said good-bye. Even her mother seemed to wipe something from her eye. When Mr Osborn had taken Rufus away Rafi looked around the house. It all seemed very quiet without Harry. She saw his water bowl sitting on the kitchen floor and she suddenly shouted, "I hate that horrible old man. I want my dog back!" and she ran upstairs to her room and sobbed.

Later that night her father came into her room. He was very gentle to her and explained that Rufus was really someone else's dog. Mr Osborn didn't have a family living at home and Rufus was all he had. Rafi had a family and her friends so she shouldn't have felt so angry at Mr Osborn.

A few days later Rafi had a letter waiting for her when she got home from school. It was from Mr Osborn. It was in shaky but clear handwriting and this is what it said.

Dear Rafi,
Thank you very much for looking after Rufus so well. I think he really enjoyed being

with you. But you have no idea how glad I am at having him back.

Perhaps you would like to help me? I can't play with Rufus like I used to because of my arthritis. Would you like to take Rufus for walks during the weekends and school holidays? I know he would like it and I would feel happier knowing that he was getting his exercise.

See you this Saturday,
Mr Osborn

It wasn't quite as good as having your own pet to cuddle up to all the time but Rafi couldn't wait until Saturday. When she called at Mr Osborn's house Rufus leapt up and down with excitement when he saw her. Rafi took him to the recreation ground to have a good run. One thing she wasn't going to do was to call him Rufus. To her he was Harry and would always be Harry.

Discussion Points
1. How did Mr Osborn know where to find Rufus?
2. Why do you think Rufus got excited when the girls called him Harry?
3. Was it right that Rafi should give up Harry?

Prayer/Reflection
Dear Lord, we are happy when things go well in our lives. We are happy when we get what our heart desires. We know that this does not always happen, so give us the strength to face our disappointments with courage, grace and humility.

Follow-up activity
Rafi had to face a big disappointment. Discuss with the children times when they have had to face disappointments. How did they cope with it? How did they feel? What words can describe these feelings? They could write a poem called, 'The Most Disappointing Time of My Life', using words that describe how they felt.

18
The Bag of Money

THEME: jumping to conclusions

Rafi came up with a novel idea for raising money for 'Children in Need'. She suggested to her friends that they should have a sponsored silence. They would go the whole day without talking! Mrs Hatch thought it was an excellent idea and she said at once that she would sponsor them. She even suggested carrying on with it till the end of term but Rafi thought that one day would be all that they could manage!

The rest of the school were allowed to wear their home clothes and not school uniform as long as they brought 50p as a donation. Some other children had other ideas for raising money such as selling old comics and making biscuits. Rafi managed to talk Delphine and Clare into joining her in the sponsored silence. As soon as the register was called the girls started their silence and spent the morning not saying a single word. Some of the others tried to trick them into saying words. George asked Clare which song she thought would win the Eurovision song contest but he was disappointed when Clare wrote her answer on a piece of paper. George then tried to trick Rafi by saying that she loved Jonny but she only stuck her tongue out at him and then ignored him. George turned to Delphine. He was determined to get one of them to talk and break their silence.

"Delphine, what's that bee doing on your head?" he whispered to her. But Delphine just smiled and wrote on a pad of paper, 'You've got a wasp up your nose!' Mrs Hatch then told George to leave the girls alone, as she was enjoying the peace and quiet.

The girls managed the whole day without talking. Lunch time was difficult as everyone started to talk to them but they stayed together as a group and made sure nobody broke their silence. When three thirty came there was a sigh of relief from everybody in the class. Even Mrs Hatch was getting fed up with the hundreds of bits of paper used for writing notes and the constant hand signals which became more annoying than talking. Mrs Hatch then wrote a note for each of the girls to say that they had completed six and a half hours of silence. That

Sometimes we are quick to accuse others of doing wrong.
Help us to make sure our judgements are sound
before we make accusations

THE BAG OF MONEY

weekend the girls collected their sponsor money from their families and friends.

When the girls met on Monday morning they put all their sponsor money in one bag. Rafi took the bag and put it onto Mrs Hatch's desk along with a note that said, 'Sponsored silence money from Rafi, Delphine and Clare'.

At morning break Rafi went up to Mrs Hatch and said, "Could we have your sponsor money for our silence, please?"

"Yes, I've got it right here," she replied. "Have you got a bag for all your money?"

"I put it on your desk this morning," said Rafi.

Mrs Hatch began to search her desk. She looked through the drawers, under books and even on the floor. "Are you sure you put it on my desk? she asked. "It doesn't seem to be here."

"We saw her put it there," said Delphine with Clare nodding her head in agreement.

"Somebody has stolen it," cried Rafi. She was so proud of her idea and how they raised the money. She wasn't too sure how much they had in total. They were going to count it at playtime.

"George was in here when we put it on your desk," said Clare, "I bet he took it."

"He's always nicking people's rubbers and pencils, he must have taken it," agreed Delphine. By this time the girls were staring at George who was minding his own business working on his maths.

"George, would you come here please?" asked Mrs Hatch. George got up from his work and walked up to the group standing around the teacher's desk. He had a puzzled look on his face, he sensed the girls were angry with him. He thought perhaps they were complaining about the way he kept trying to make them talk last Friday.

"Were you in the classroom before morning whistle?" asked Mrs Hatch.
during   break

"Yes," said George hesitantly, he was really puzzled now, "I came in to get my football."

and she turned & pointed her finger straight at George.

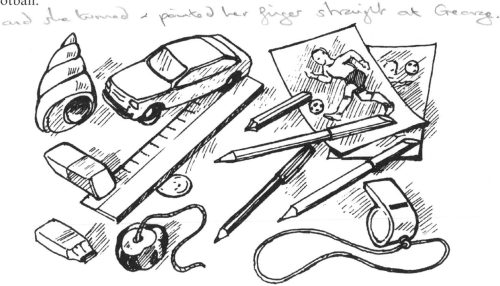

"Did you see a bag a money on my desk?"

"I saw Rafi put something on your desk," said George, "I didn't know what it was."

"Liar!" shouted Rafi.

I bet you did

"Give us our money," demanded Delphine. The rest of the class stopped working and stared at what was happening.

"I haven't got your stupid money!" shouted George back.

"Can we search his tray?" asked Clare.

"That's not fair," said George and he was now getting quite upset.

"George is right," said Mrs Hatch. "Just because he was in here doesn't mean he took your money." But Rafi wasn't listening, she went over to the trays, pulled out George's and began to search it. In no time at all she had emptied George's tray and all his things were spread over the floor, but there was no sign of the money.

Mrs Hatch was very cross with Rafi, "I think you had better put all of George's things back into his tray. You are being very unfair!"

At that precise moment Mrs Roberts, the school secretary, came in.

"I'm sorry Mrs Hatch, I took this bag of money by mistake when I was collecting the dinner money." She put the bag containing the sponsor money on the desk and walked out.

The girls went red with embarrassment. George breathed a sigh of relief and then looked really angry. The rest of the class held their breath to see what was going to happen next!

Discussion Points

1. What do you think should happen next?
2. Why was George instantly blamed?
3. The girls jumped to conclusions. What should they have done first before blaming George?
4. What do you think of the way Mrs Hatch behaved towards George?
5. There is a phrase 'give a dog a bad name'. How does this relate to the story above? What can people with bad reputations do to change people's perceptions of them?

Prayer/Reflection

Lord, help us to make the right decisions in our lives. Teach us to be kind and caring and to have the strength to say sorry when we hurt somebody by our foolish actions.

Follow-up Activity

Ask the children to make a list of their feelings when they have been accused of something they did not do. Ask them to draw a picture of themselves not looking very happy and write these words on the picture.